I Love You,
I Love You

By Jennifer Dawn

All rights reserved. No part of this publication may be reproduced, stored in a retrieval system or transmitted in any form or by any means – electronic, mechanical, photocopying, and recording or otherwise – without the prior written permission of the author, except for brief passages quoted by a reviewer in a newspaper or magazine. To perform any of the above is an infringement of copyright law.

ISBN –   978-0-9936204-4-7

To my son, I Love You

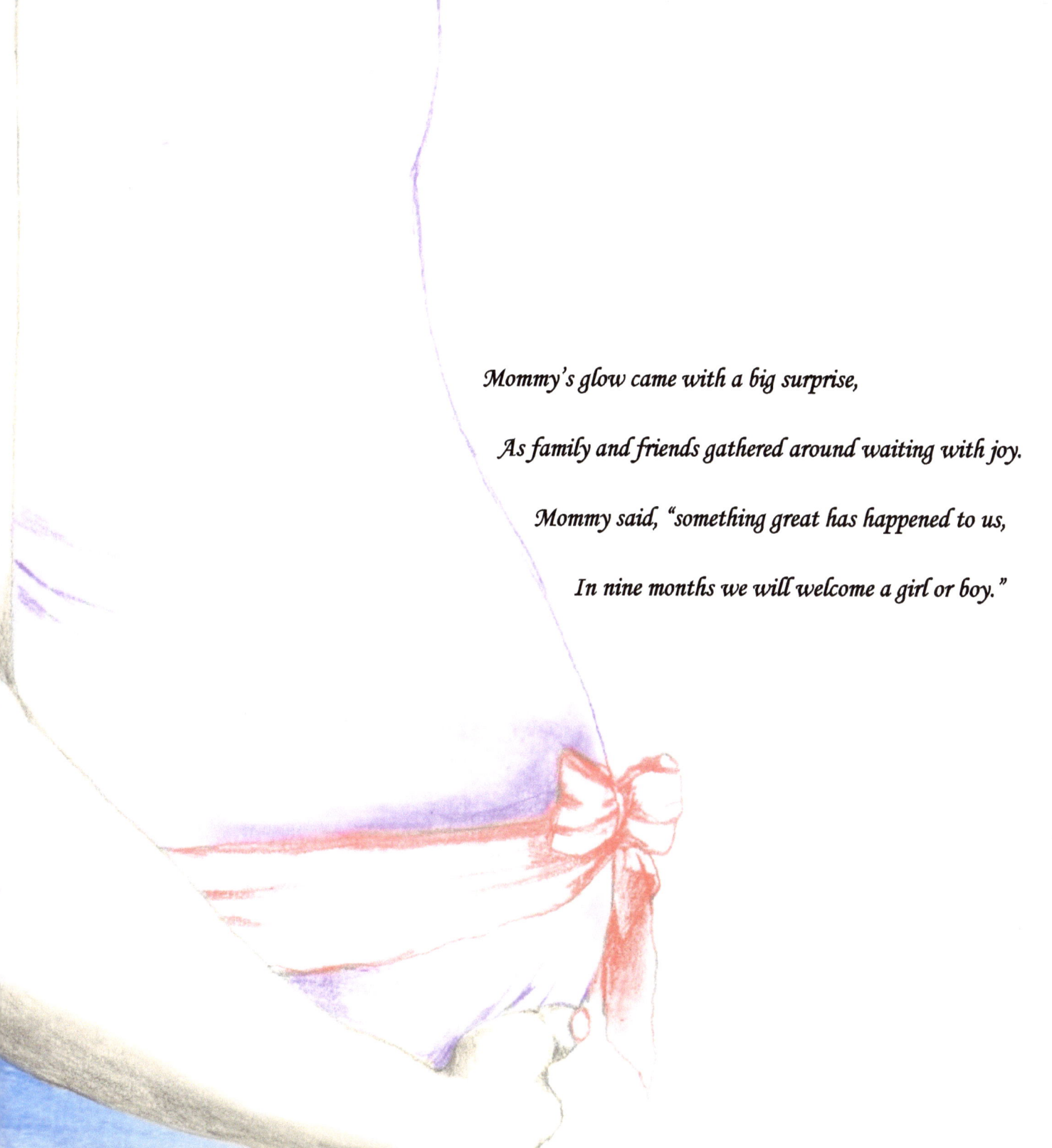

Mommy's glow came with a big surprise,

As family and friends gathered around waiting with joy.

Mommy said, "something great has happened to us,

In nine months we will welcome a girl or boy."

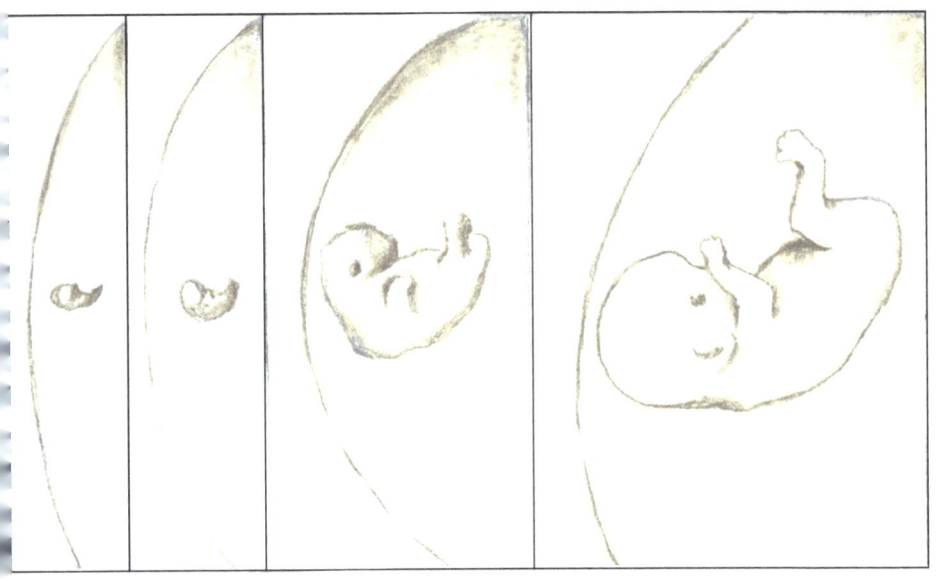

Nine months of changes

And a few hours of labour,

There were moments of pain,

But the enjoyment is forever.

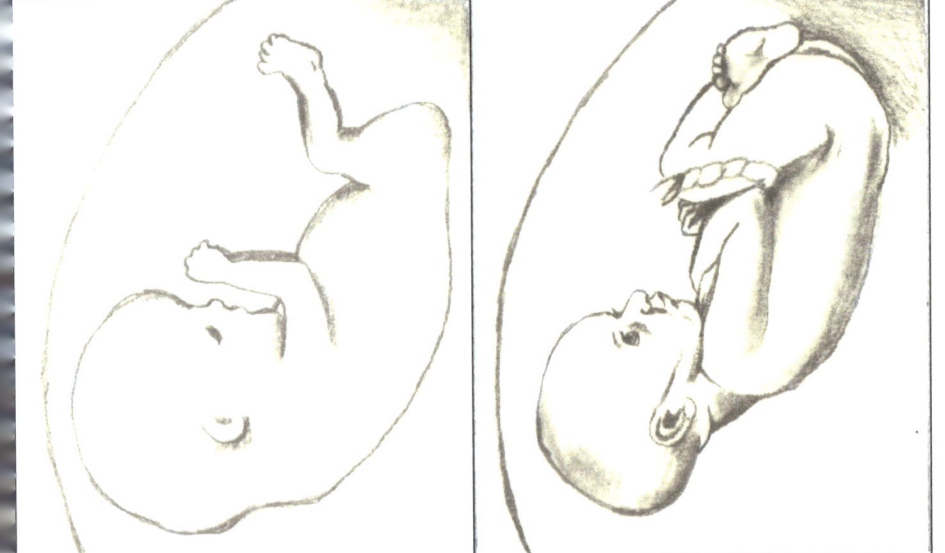

(Sing)

(Parent) I love you,

(Child) I love you,

(Parent) You're the start of another generation,

(Parent) I love you,

(Child) I love you,

(Parent) Our adorable creation,

(Parent) I love you!

When you find your purpose in life,

Do it with your heart and soul.

Live, love, learn,

And I will teach you control.

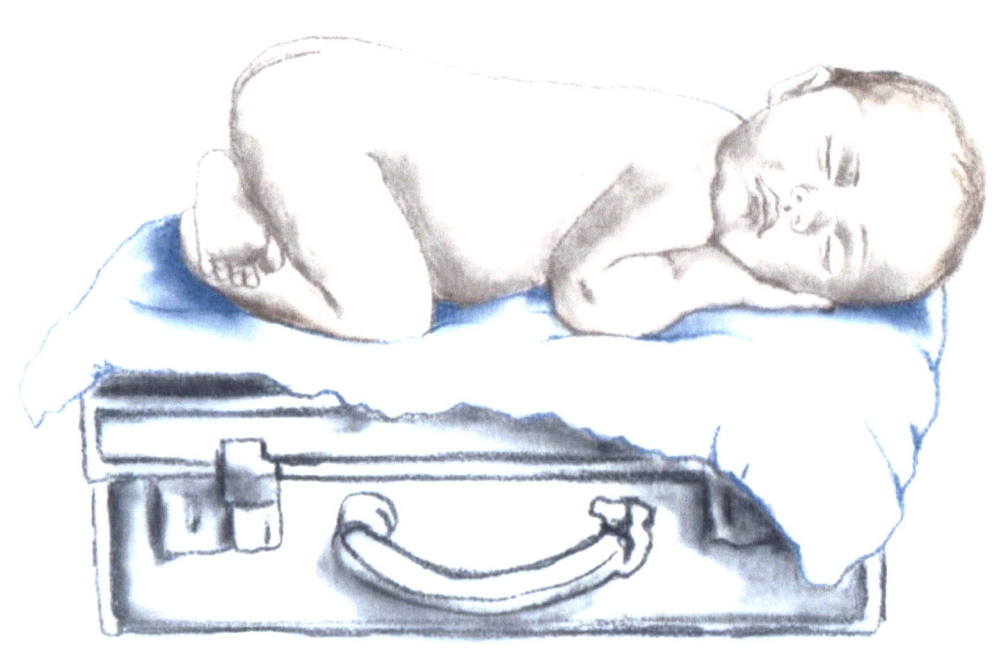

You had the cutest little smile

And had so many funny giggles.

When we played music,

You showed off your wiggles.

I love you,

I love you,

You're the start of another generation,

I love you,

I love you,

Our adorable creation,

I love you!

You will taste your first food,

And make funny faces.

It's happening so quick,

Next, you will be tying your laces.

The stages of change

Both happy and sad,

Is a learning experience

For Mom and Dad.

I love you,

I love you,

You're the start of another generation,

I love you,

I love you,

Our adorable creation,

I love you!

You will learn to walk and talk

And create your own identity,

Meeting a variety of people along the way

And treating everyone with equality.

As you grow older,

I will teach you safety and awareness.

You will learn from your own mistakes,

But remember, never to be careless.

I love you,

I love you,

You're the start of another generation,

I love you,

I love you,

Our adorable creation,

I love you!

You will meet new friends,

And some will be funny and kind.

But one day you will meet a bully,

Please always tell me what's on your mind.

I will always be here for you,

No matter what you want to say.

It's important to talk to me,

At any time, and, on any day.

I love you,

I love you,

You're the start of another generation,

I love you,

I love you,

Our adorable creation,

I love you!

You will go through school,

And Mommy and Daddy will cry.

Seeing our little baby growing up,

Like a butterfly…sigh.

As your parents grow, so shall you,

I can't believe it's happening so fast.

Appreciate all of your memories,

And remember, you can always learn from your past.

I love you,

I love you,

You're the start of another generation,

I love you,

I love you,

Our adorable creation,

I love you!

Your gown and cap came too soon,

It's time for you to go your own way.

Please never forget me,

I will be just a phone call away.

Make sure you are always respectful,

Work hard in life, and enjoy the sun.

There will be ups, and there will be downs,

But always take time for some fun.

I love you,

I love you,

You're the start of another generation,

I love you,

I love you,

Our adorable creation,

I love you!

One day you will fall in love,

And our family will happily grow.

Love is the greatest gift you can give,

What you do today creates your tomorrow.

One day I will look down from above,

And you may feel torn apart.

Stay strong and cherish our memories,

I will always be in your heart.

I love you,

I love you,

You're the start of another generation,

I love you,

I love you,

Our adorable creation,

I love you!

Get in touch with us below!

www.ingramcontent.com/pod-product-compliance
Lightning Source LLC
Chambersburg PA
CBHW041236040426
42444CB00003B/179